The
HIEROGLYPHIC
Catalog

please consider leaving a review.

Organization

Each page is organized into ten rows, with each row containing four cells: Sign, Gardiner's Number, Unicode, and Description.

	**G45** **13174**	Combination of (G43) and (D36). Phono wʿ.In wʿw "soldier."

Phono. – Phonogram   Det. – Determinative
Ideo. – Ideogram   Var. – Variant.

Table of Contents

Transliteration table

Hieroglyph	Gardiner No.	Transliteration	Pronunciation	As In
	G1	ꜣ or 3	a	Father
	M17	i̓	i	Machine
	Z4	y	y	Yes
	M17-M17	y	y	Yes
	D36	ꜥ	a	Father
	G43	w	w	Wet
	D58	b	b	Bat
	Q3	p	p	Pat
	I9	f	f	Fun
	G17	m	m	Mat
	N35	n	n	Net
	D21	r	r	Red
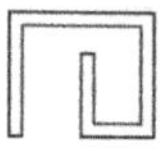	O4	h	h	Hat
	V28	ḥ	h	Hat
	Aa1	ḫ	kh	Scottish "loch"
	F32	ẖ	kh	Scottish "loch"
	O34	s (z)	z	Zebra
	S29	s (ś)	sh	She
	N27	š	sh	She
	N29	ḳ	q	Quick
	V31	k	k	Kite
	W11	g	g	Goat
	X1	t	t	Top
	V13	ṯ	th	Think
	D46	d	d	Dog
	I10	ḏ	th	This

	A1 / 13000	Seated man. Det. of man, names; Pronoun 1st sing. i, wi, ink, kwi. "I," "me," "my."
	A2 / 13001	Seated man with hand to mouth. Det. of eat, drink, speak, think.
	A3 / 13002	Man sitting on heel. Det. of sit.
	A4 / 13003	Seated man with hands raised. Det. adoration, hide
	A5 / 13004	Crouching man hiding behind wall. Det. hide
	A5A / 13005	Seated man hiding behind wall.
	A6 / 13006	Seated man under vase from which water flows. Det. purity, cleanliness
	A6A / 13007	Seated man reaching for libation stone, under vase from which water flows.
	A6B / 13008	Seated man reaching down, under vase from which water flows.
	A7 / 13009	Fatigued man. Det. weary, weak

A8 1300A	Man performing hnw-rite. Det. in hnw "jubilation"
A9 1300B	Seated man with ▽ (W10) on head. Det. in 3ṯp "load," f3i "carry," k3t "work."
A10 1300C	Seated man holding oar. Det. in sḳdw "sail."
A11 1300D	Seated man holding (S42) and (S39). Det. ḫnms "friend."
A12 1300E	Soldier with bow and quiver. Det. mšʿ "army," soldier.
A13 1300F	Man with arms tied behind his back. Det. ḫfty "enemy."
A14 13010	Falling man with blood streaming from his head. Det. of mwt "die," enemy.
A14A 13011	Man whose head is hit with an axe. Var. of A14
A15 13012	Man falling. Det. ḫr "fall," sḫrt "overthrow."
A16 13013	Man bowing down. Det. ksi "bow."

| | A17 | Child sitting with hand to mouth. |
| | 13014 | Det. šri "young." Ideo. ẖrd "child." |

| | A17A | Child sitting with arms hanging down. |
| | 13015 | Det. sit, young. |

| | A18 | Child wearing ⚲ (S3). |
| | 13016 | Det. child-king |

| | A19 | Bent man leaning on staff. |
| | 13017 | Det. i3w "old," smsw "eldest," wr "great one, chief." |

| | A20 | Man leaning on forked staff. |
| | 13018 | Var. of A19. |

| | A21 | Man holding staff with handkerchief. |
| | 13019 | Det. and Ideo. sr "official, noble." |

| | A22 | Statue of man with staff and ⚲ (S42). |
| | 1301A | Det. statue. |

| | A23 | King with staff and ⚲ (T3). |
| | 1301B | Det. ity, "sovereign." |

| | A24 | Man striking with both hands. |
| | 1301C | Det. ḥwi, "strike," nḥm "take away." Ideo. nḫt strong. |

| | A25 | Man striking, with left arm hanging behind back. |
| | 1301D | Det. ḥwi "strike." |

A26	1301E	Man with one arm pointing forward. Det. nis "call." Ideo. vocative i, "Oh!"
A27	1301F	Hastening man. Phon. in "by," agent particle.
A28	13020	Man with hands raised on either side. Det. ḳ3 "high," ḥʻi "rejoice."
A29	13021	Man upside down. Det. upside down.
A30	13022	Man with hands raised in front. Det. i3w "praise," dw3 "adoration."
A31	13023	Man with hands raised behind him. Det. turn away.
A32	13024	Man dancing with arms to the back. Det. dance.
A32A	13025	Man dancing with arms to the front.
A33	13026	Man with stick and bundle on shoulder. Det. wander, herdsman.
A34	13027	Man pounding in a mortar. Det. ḫwsi "pound, build."

| | A35 | Man building wall. |
| | 13028 | Det. and Ideo. ḳd "build." |

| | A36 | Man kneading into vessel. |
| | 13029 | Det. and Ideo. ʿfty "brewer." |

| | A37 | Man in vessel. |
| | 1302A | Use as A36. |

| | A38 | Man holding necks of two emblematic animals with panther heads. |
| | 1302B | Ideo. ḳis/ḳsi ""Cusae" (town). |

| | A39 | Man on two giraffes. |
| | 1302C | Use as A38. |

| | A40 | Seated god. |
| | 1302D | Det. god. Replaces A1 as 1st sing pronoun when god speaks. i, wi, ink, kwi. |

| | A40A | Seated god with ⌐ (S40). |
| | 1302E | |

| | A41 | King with uraeus. |
| | 1302F | Det. nsw "king," ḥm "majesty," nb "lord." |

| | A42 | King with uraeus and ⌐ (S45). |
| | 13030 | Use as A41. |

| | A42A | King with uraeus and ⌐ (S45). |
| | 13031 | |

| | A43 | King wearing (S1). |
| | 13032 | Det. king of Upper Egypt. |

| | A43A | King wearing (S1) with (S40). |
| | 13033 | |

| | A44 | King wearing (S1) with (S45). |
| | 13034 | Use as A43. |

| | A45 | King wearing (S3). |
| | 13035 | Det. and Ideo. bity "king of Lower Egypt." |

| | A45A | King wearing (S3) with (S40). |
| | 13036 | |

| | A46 | King wearing (S3) with (S45). |
| | 13037 | Same as A45 |

| | A47 | Shepherd seated and wrapped in mantle, holding stick. |
| | 13038 | Det. and Ideo. s3w "guard," mniw "herdsman." |

| | A48 | Beardless man seated and holding knife. |
| | 13039 | Det. iry "relating to." |

| | A49 | Seated Syrian holding stick. |
| | 1303A | Det. foreigner, ʿ3mw "Asiatics." |

| | A50 | Noble on chair. |
| | 1303B | Det. revered person, deceased. Var. A1 for 1st sing. pronoun. |

| | A51 | Noble on chair with ⋀ (S45). |
| | 1303C | Det. and Ideo. špsi "noble" |

| | A52 | Noble squatting with ⋀ (S45). |
| | 1303D | Det. revered person, deceased. |

| | A53 | Standing mummy. |
| | 1303E | Det. mummy, statue, likeness, form. |

| | A54 | Lying mummy. |
| | 1303F | Det. dead. |

| | A55 | Mummy on bed. |
| | 13040 | Det. sḏr "lie down," dead. |

| | A56 | Seated man holding stick. |
| | 13041 | |

| | A57 | Man holding ⌂ (R4). |
| | 13042 | |

| | A58 | Man applying hoe to ground. |
| | 13043 | |

| | A59 | Man threatening with stick. |
| | 13044 | Det. drive off. |

| | A60 | Man sowing seeds. |
| | 13045 | |

	A61	Man looking over his shoulder.
	13046	
	A62	Asiatic.
	13047	
	A63	King on throne holding staff.
	13048	
	A64	Man sitting on heels holding forward ▽ (W10).
	13049	
	A65	Man wearing tunic with fringes and holding mace.
	1304A	
	A66	Man holding 🏺 (Y8).
	1304B	
	A67	Dwarf.
	1304C	
	A68	Man holding up knife.
	1304D	
	A69	Seated man with raised right arm and left arm hanging down.
	1304E	
	A70	Seated man with raised arms.
	1304F	

	B1	Seated woman.
	13050	Det. woman, name. Sometimes for A1 1st sing. pronoun – i
	B2	Pregnant woman.
	13051	Det. pregnant
	B3	Woman giving birth.
	13052	Det. and Ideo. msi "give birth, bear."
	B4	Combination of (B3) and (F31).
	13053	Use as B3.
	B5	Woman suckling child.
	13054	Det. mn't "nurse."
	B5A	Woman suckling child (simplified).
	13055	
	B6	Woman on chair with child on lap.
	13056	Det. rnn "nurse."
	B7	Queen wearing diadem and holding flower.
	13057	Det. queens' names.
	B8	Woman holding (M9).
	13058	
	B9	Woman holding (Y8).
	13059	

	C1 1305A	God with 𓇲 (N6). Det. and Ideo. Rˁ "Re, sun-god"
	C2 1305B	God with head of falcon with sun on head and holding ♀ (S34). Var. C1. Det. and Ideo. Rˁ "Re, sun-god"
	C2A 1305C	God with head of falcon with sun on head.
	C2B 1305D	(C2A) reversed.
	C2C 1305E	(C2) reversed.
	C3 1305F	God with head of ibis. Det. or Ideo. ḏḥwty "Thoth"
	C4 13060	God with head of ram. Det. or Ideo. ẖnmw "Khnum"
	C5 13061	God with head of ram holding ♀ (S34). Use as C4.
	C6 13062	God with head of jackal. Det. and Ideo. inpw "Anubis," wp-w3wt "Wepwawet."
	C7 13063	God with head of Seth-animal. Det. and Ideo. Stẖ "Seth."

	C8	Ithyphallic god with ⧘ (S9), uplifted arm and ⧋ (S45).
	13064	Det. and Ideo. Mnw "Min."
	C9	Goddess with sun and horns.
	13065	Det. and Ideo.
	C10	Goddess with feather on head.
	13066	Det. and Ideo. M3ˁt "Maat"
	C10A	Goddess with feather on head holding ⧜ (S34).
	13067	Use as C10
	C11	God with arms supporting (the sky) and ⧝ (M4) on head.
	13068	Ideo. ḥḥ "million," god Heh.
	C12	God with ⧘ (S9) and ⧞ (S40).
	13069	Det. and Ideo. Imn "Amun."
	C13	⧟ (C12) reversed.
	1306A	
	C14	God with ⧘ (S9) and ⧠ (T16A).
	1306B	
	C15	⧡ (C14) reversed.
	1306C	
	C16	God wearing ⧢ (S3) with ⧜ (S34).
	1306D	

| | C17 | God with head of falcon and / (S9). |
| | 1306E | Det. and Ideo Mnṯw "Montu." |

| | C18 | Squatting god. |
| | 1306F | Det. and Ideo. t3-ṯnnii "Tatjenen." |

| | C19 | Mummy-shaped god. |
| | 13070 | Det. and Ideo. Ptḥ "Ptah." |

| | C20 | Mummy-shaped god in shrine. |
| | 13071 | Use as C19 |

| | C21 | Bes. |
| | 13072 | |

| | C22 | God with head of falcon and moon disk. |
| | 13073 | |

| | C23 | Goddess with head of feline and (N6). |
| | 13074 | |

| | C24 | God wearing (S3) with (S40). |
| | 13075 | |

| | D1 | Head in profile. |
| | 13076 | Phono. tp. Det. or Ideo. for tp "head," tpy "first, chief." Det. ḏ3ḏ3 "head." |

| | D2 | Face. |
| | 13077 | Phon. ḥr. Ideo. for ḥr "face." |

	D3	Hair.
	13078	Det. for šny "hair," iwn "complexion, nature." Abbr. for gm wš "found missing."
	D4	Eye.
	13079	Phono. iri "to do, make." Ideo. for irt "eye."
	D5	Eye touched up with paint.
	1307A	Det. for actions or conditions of the eye. ex. dgi "look," šp "blind."
	D6	Eye with painted upper lid.
	1307B	Use as D5.
	D7	Eye with painted lower lid.
	1307C	Det. for adorn and in ʿnw " "Anu" (location).
	D8	Eye enclosed in ___ (N18).
	1307D	Det. for ʿnw "Turah," ʿn "beautiful."
	D8A	Eye with painted lower lid enclosed in ___ (N18).
	1307E	
	D9	Eye with flowing tears.
	1307F	Det. or Ideo. for rmi "weep."
	D10	WDAt-eye.
	13080	Det. or Ideo. for w3ḏt "wedjat eye."
	D11	Left part of white of (D10).
	13081	1/2 ḥeqat measure of grain.

D12 / 13082	Pupil of eye. Det. for ḏfd "pupil of eye."	
D13 / 13083	Eye-brow. 1/8 ḥeqat measure of grain.	
D14 / 13084	Right part of white of ⟨eye⟩ (D10). 1/16 ḥeqat measure of grain.	
D15 / 13085	Diagonal marking of ⟨eye⟩ (D10). 1/32 ḥeqat measure of grain.	
D16 / 13086	Vertical marking of ⟨eye⟩ (D10). 1/64 ḥeqat measure of grain.	
D17 / 13087	Combination of (D16) and (D15). Det. or Ideo. for tit "figure, image."	
D18 / 13088	Ear. Det. or Ideo. for msḏr "ear."	
D19 / 13089	Nose, eye and cheek. Det. or Ideo. for fnd "nose." Det. sn "smell," rš "rejoice."	
D20 / 1308A	Nose, eye and cheek in semi-cursive form. Use as D19	
D21 / 1308B	Mouth. Phon. r. Ideo. for r "mouth."	

| | D22 | Mouth with two strokes. |
| | 1308C | Ideo. for rwy "2/3." |

| | D23 | Mouth with three strokes. |
| | 1308D | Ideo. for ḫmt rw "3/4." |

| | D24 | Upper lip with teeth. |
| | 1308E | Det. or Ideo. for spt "lip." Mistakenly used a F42. |

| | D25 | Lips with teeth. |
| | 1308F | Det. or Ideo. for spty "lips." |

| | D26 | Liquid issuing from lips. |
| | 13090 | Det. for spit, spew. ex. psg "spit," ḳꜥ "spew out." |

| | D27 | Small breast. |
| | 13091 | Det. for breast, suckle. ex. mnḏ "breast" |

| | D27A | Large breast. |
| | 13092 | Use as D27. |

| | D28 | Arms in kA-posture. |
| | 13093 | Phono. k3. Ideo. for k3 "soul." |

| | D29 | Combination of (D28) and (R12). |
| | 13094 | Use as D28. |

| | D30 | (D28) with tail. |
| | 13095 | Det. for nḥb-k3w "Uniter of Attributes, Assigner of Kas," name of mythical serpent deity. |

| | D31 | Combination of ⟨⟩ (D32) and ⟨⟩ (U36). |
| | 13096 | Ideo. for ḥm-k3 "ka servent." |

| | D31A | Combination of ⟨⟩ (D28) and ⟨⟩ (U36). |
| | 13097 | |

| | D32 | Arms embracing. |
| | 13098 | Det. for embrace, open. ex. inḳ "envelop," ḥpt "embrace." |

| | D33 | Arms rowing. |
| | 13099 | Phono. ẖn. Ideo. for ẖni "row." |

| | D34 | Arms holding shield and battle-axe. |
| | 1309A | Ideo. for ʿḥ3 "fight" |

| | D34A | Arms holding shield and mace. |
| | 1309B | Use as D34. |

| | D35 | Arms in gesture of negation. |
| | 1309C | Phono. n. Ideo. for n and nn, "not." Det. negation. |

| | D36 | Forearm. |
| | 1309D | Phono. ʿ. Ideo. ʿ "arm, hand." |

| | D37 | Forearm with ⟨⟩ (X8). |
| | 1309E | Phono. di in rdi "give." |

| | D38 | Forearm with rounded loaf. |
| | 1309F | Phono. mi or m. Det. for imi "give." |

	D39 / **130A0**	Forearm with ◌ (W24). Det. for offer, present. ex. ḥnk "present," drp "offer."
	D40 / **130A1**	Forearm with stick. Det. for force, effort. ex. nḫt "strong." Ideo. h3i "evaluate."
	D41 / **130A2**	Forearm with palm down and bent upper arm. Phono. ni. Det. for arm. ex. rmn "arm, shoulder."
	D42 / **130A3**	Forearm with palm down and straight upper arm. Det. or Ideo. for mḥ "cubit"
	D43 / **130A4**	Forearm with ⋀ (S45). Phono. ḫw. Ideo. for ḫwi "protect.
	D44 / **130A5**	Forearm with ⎀ (S42). Det. and Ideo. for ḫrp "control, be at head of, administer."
	D45 / **130A6**	Arm with nHbt-wand. Det. and Ideo. for ḏsr "clear road, sacred, holy."
	D46 / **130A7**	Hand. Phono. d. Ideo. for ḏrt "hand."
	D46A / **130A8**	Liquid falling from hand. Ideo. for idt "fragrance."
	D47 / **130A9**	Hand with palm up. Det. for ḏrt "hand" when spelled with Phono.

	D48 / **130AA**	Hand without thumb. Ideo. šsp "palm, hand-breadth" (measure)
	D48A / **130AB**	Hand holding an egg.
	D49 / **130AC**	Fist. Det. for grasp. ex. 3mm "grasp," ḫf' "seize."
	D50 / **130AD**	Finger vertically. Ideo. for ḏb' "finger," ḏb' "10,000." Det. for accurate, when doubled.
	D50A / **130AE**	....
	D50B / **130AF**	....
	D50C / **130B0**	....
	D50D / **130B1**	....
	D50E / **130B2**	....
	D50F / **130B3**	....

	D50G / **130B4**	....
	D50H / **130B5**	....
	D50I / **130B6**	....
	D51 / **130B7**	Finger horizontally. Det. for actions related to finger, fruit, flower. ex. ʿnt "nail," ḫ3i "measure," dḳr "fruit."
	D52 / **130B8**	Phallus. Phono. mt. Det. for male. ex. ʿ3 "ass," t̲3y "male." Ideo. k3 "bull."
	D52A / **130B9**	Combination of ⌐ (D52) and ∏ (S29).
	D53 / **130BA**	Liquid issuing from phallus. Det. for male, penis. ex. m b3ḥ "in the presence of" d̲r b3ḥ "since," r b3ḥ "before."
	D54 / **130BB**	Legs walking. Phono. iw in iwi "come." Det. for motion.
	D54A / **130BC**	Hieratic legs walking.
	D55 / **130BD**	Legs walking backwards. Det. for backwards. ex. ʿnn "turn back," ḫtḫt "be reversed."

	D56	Leg.
	130BE	Phono. pd. Det. for leg, foot. ex. rd "leg," pd "knee."
	D57	Combination of (D56) and (T30).
	130BF	Det. for mutilate. ex. i3ṯ "be mutilated."
	D58	Foot.
	130C0	Phono. b. Ideo. for bw "place."
	D59	Combination of (D58) and (D36).
	130C1	Phono. ʿb
	D60	(D58) under vase from which water flows.
	130C2	Ideo. for wʿb "pure, clean."
	D61	Three toes oriented leftward.
	130C3	Ideo. for s3ḥ "toe"
	D62	Three toes oriented rightward.
	130C4	Use as D61.
	D63	Two toes oriented leftward.
	130C5	Use as D61.
	D64	Hand with palm down.
	130C6	
	D65	Lock of hair.
	130C7	

| 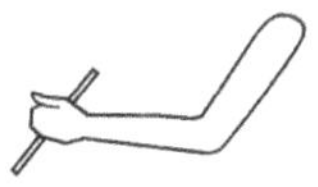 | D66 | Arm with reed pen. |
| | 130C8 | |

|  | D67 | Dot. |
| | 130C9 | |

| | D67A | .... |
| | 130CA | |

| | D67B | .... |
| | 130CB | |

| | D67C | .... |
| | 130CC | |

| | D67D | .... |
| | 130CD | |

| | D67E | .... |
| | 130CE | |

| | D67F | .... |
| | 130CF | |

| | D67G | .... |
| | 130D0 | |

| | D67H | .... |
| | 130D1 | |

	E1 130D2	Bull. Det. of cattle. ex. ng "bull," mnmnt "cattle." Ideo. in k3 "bull."
	E2 130D3	Bull charging. Det. in sm3 "fighting bull." Ideo. in k3 nḫt "victorious bull," (epithet of Pharaoh.)
	E3 130D4	Calf. Det. in bḫs "calf"
	E4 130D5	Sacred HsAt-cow. Det. in ḥs3t "sacred cow."
	E5 130D6	Cow suckling calf. Det. in 3ms "show solicitude."
	E6 130D7	Horse. Ideo. or Det. in ssmt "horse." Det. in ibr "stallion."
	E7 130D8	Donkey. Det. in ꜥ3 "donkey."
	E8 130D9	Kid. Phon. ib, "kid." Det. in ꜥwt "flocks."
	E8A 130DA	Kid jumping.
	E9 130DB	Newborn bubalis or hartebeest. Phon. iw. In iwr "conceive."

	E9A / **130DC**	Mature bovine lying down.
	E10 / **130DD**	Ram. Det. in b3 "ram," ḫnmw "Khnum," ʿwt ḥḏt "white flocks, sheep"
	E11 / **130DE**	Ram. Use as E10
	E12 / **130DF**	Pig. Det. in rri "pig."
	E13 / **130E0**	Cat. Det. in miw "cat."
	E14 / **130E1**	Dog (saluki). Det. in iw "dog," ṯsm "hound."
	E15 / **130E2**	Lying canine. Det. or Ideo. in Inpw, "Anubis."
	E16 / **130E3**	Lying canine on shrine. Use as E15.
	E16A / **130E4**	Lying canine on shrine with (S45).
	E17 / **130E5**	Jackal. Det. or Ideo. in s3b "jackal" and "dignitary."

	E17A	Jackal looking back.
	130E6	
	E18	Wolf on ⬩ (R12) with SdSd.
	130E7	Det. or Ideo. in Wp-w3wt "Opener of ways, Wepwawet."
	E19	Combination of ⬩ (E19) and ⬩ (T3).
	130E8	Use as E18
	E20	Seth-animal.
	130E9	Det. or Ideo. in sth, stš "Seth." Det. in ḫnnw "turmoil," sh3 "confusion."
	E20A	Combination of ⬩ (E20) and ⬩ (V30).
	130EA	
	E21	Lying Seth-animal.
	130EB	Det. in nšni "storm, rage."
	E22	Lion.
	130EC	Det. or Ideo. in m3i "lion"
	E23	Lying lion.
	130ED	Phon. rw. Det. or Ideo. in rw "lion."
	E24	Panther.
	130EE	Det. or Ideo. in 3by "panther, leopard."
	E25	Hippopotamus.
	130EF	Det. in db, dib "hippopotamus."

| | E26 | Elephant. |
| | 130F0 | Det. 3bw "elephant." Ideo. in 3bw "Elephantine." |

| | E27 | Giraffe. |
| | 130F1 | Det. sr "foretell." Det. or Ideo in mmi "giraffe." |

| | E28 | Oryx. |
| | 130F2 | Det. in m3ḥḏ "oryx." |

| | E28A | Combination of (E28), (N24) and some type of jar. |
| | 130F3 | |

| | E29 | Gazelle. |
| | 130F4 | Det. in gḥs "gazelle." |

| | E30 | Ibex. |
| | 130F5 | Det. in n3w, nr3w, ni3 "ibex." |

| | E31 | Goat with collar. |
| | 130F6 | Det. in sꜥḥ "rank, privilege." |

| | E32 | Baboon. |
| | 130F7 | Det. in iꜥn "baboon," ky "monkey," qnd "furious." |

| | E33 | Monkey. |
| | 130F8 | Det. gf, gif "monkey." |

| | E34 | Hare. |
| | 130F9 | Phono. wn. wnn "be." |

| | E34A | Hare (low). |
| | 130FA | |

| | E36 | Baboon. |
| | 130FB | |

| | E37 | Combination of (E36), (V36) and (V30). |
| | 130FC | |

| | E38 | Long-horned bull. |
| | 130FD | |

| | F1 | Head of ox. |
| | 130FE | Ideo. in offering formulas for k3 "cattle." |

| | F1A | Head of bovine. |
| | 130FF | |

| | F2 | Head of charging ox. |
| | 13100 | Det. in ḏnd "rage." |

| | F3 | Head of hippopotamus. |
| | 13101 | Phono. 3t. Det. or Ideo. in "moment, attack." |

| | F4 | Forepart of lion. |
| | 13102 | Ideo. in ḥ3t "front," ḥ3ty "heart." |

| | F5 | Head of bubalis or hartebeest. |
| | 13103 | Phon. šs3. Det. and Ideo. in šs3 "skilled" and "prayer." |

F6 13104	Forepart of bubalis or hartebeest. Use as F5
F7 13105	Head of ram. Det. in šft "ram's head." Det. or Ideo. in šfyt "worth, dignity."
F8 13106	Forepart of ram. Use as F7
F9 13107	Head of leopard. Det. or Ideo. in pḥty "strength."
F10 13108	Head and neck of animal. Det. in ḫḫ "throat," ʿm "swallow."
F11 13109	Head and neck of animal. Use as F10
F12 1310A	Head and neck of canine. Phon. wsr. Ideo in wsrt "neck." In wsr "powerful"
F13 1310B	Horns. Phon. wp. Ideo. in wpt "brow, beginning."
F13A 1310C	Horns (low).
F14 1310D	Combination of ∪ (F13) and ∤ (M4). Ideo. wpt-rnpt "Opening of the Year."

F15 / 1310E	Combination of 𓆦 (F14) and ⊙ (N5). Use as F14	
F16 / 1310F	Horn. Phono. ʿb. Det. or Ideo. in db "horn," ʿb "horn." In m-ʿb "together with."	
F17 / 13110	Combination of ﹍ (F16) with vase from which water flows. Det. or Ideo. in ʿbw "purification."	
F18 / 13111	Tusk. Phono. bḥ, ḥw. Det. and Ideo. in ibḥ "tooth." Det. in sbḥ "cry."	
F19 / 13112	Lower jaw-bone of ox. Det. in ʿrt "jaw."	
F20 / 13113	Tongue. Phono. ns. In ns "tongue." Ideo. in imy-r "overseer."	
F21 / 13114	Ear of bovine. Phono. sḏm, idn. Det. or Ideo. in msḏr "ear. Ideo. sḏm, "hear."	
F21A / 13115	Hieratic ear of bovine.	
F22 / 13116	Hind-quarters of lion. Phono. pḥ in "reach," pḥty "strength." Ideo. for pḥwy "end."	
F23 / 13117	Foreleg of ox. Det. or Ideo. in ḫpš "strong arm, leg."	

	F24		⌇ (F23) reversed.
	13118		Use as F23.
	F25		Leg of ox.
	13119		Phono. wḥm in "hoof," "repeat."
	F26		Skin of goat.
	1311A		Phono. ẖn. In ẖnw "interior," ẖn "approach."
	F27		Skin of cow with bent tail.
	1311B		Det. in dḥr "hide," msk3 "skin."
	F28		Skin of cow with straight tail.
	1311C		Phono. s3b.
	F29		Cow's skin pierced by arrow.
	1311D		Phono. st. Det. and Ideo. sti "pierce, shoot."
	F30		Water-skin.
	1311E		Phono. šd. In šdi "draw forth," šdw "water skin."
	F31		Three skins tied together.
	1311F		Phono. ms. In msi "give birth."
	F31A		Three skins tied together (simplified).
	13120		
	F32		Animal's belly.
	13121		Phono. ẖ. Ideo. in ẖt "belly, body."

F33 13122	Tail. Phono. sd. Det. and Ideo in sd "tail."
F34 13123	Heart. Ideo. in ib "heart." Det. of " ḥ3ty "heart."
F35 13124	Heart and windpipe. Phono. nfr. In nfr "good, beautiful."
F36 13125	Lung and windpipe. Phono. sm3. In sm3 "unite" and "lung."
F37 13126	Backbone and ribs and spinal cord. Det. or Ideo. in i3t "back." Det. in psd "back."
F37A 13127	Backbone and ribs.
F38 13128	Backbone and ribs. Det. in psd "back."
F38A 13129	Backbone and ribs and spinal cord.
F39 1312A	Backbone and spinal cord. Det. and Ideo. in im3ḫ "spine" and "honor."
F40 1312B	Backbone and spinal cords. Phono. 3w.

F41 / 1312C	Vertebrae.	Det. in psd "back."
F42 / 1312D	Rib.	Phono. spr. In spr "approach."
F43 / 1312E	Ribs.	Det. in sḥpt "ribs."
F44 / 1312F	Leg-bone with meat.	Phono. iwꜥ, isw. In iwꜥ inherit," siw "exchange."
F45 / 13130	Uterus.	Det. or Ideo. in dit "vulva, cow."
F45A / 13131	Uterus (simplified).	
F46 / 13132	Intestine.	Ideo. in q3b "instestine," m-q3b "in the midst of" pḫr "turn."
F46A / 13133	Intestine.	
F47 / 13134	Intestine.	Use as F46.
F47A / 13135	Intestine.	

	F48 / 13136	Intestine. Use as F46.
	F49 / 13137	Intestine. Use as F46.
	F50 / 13138	Combination of ⬭ (F46) and ⎅ (S29). Phono. spḫr, "write, copy."
	F51 / 13139	Piece of flesh. Phono. is, ist, ws. Det. ḥꜥ "flesh," iwf "meat."
	F51A / 1313A	Three pieces of flesh horizontally.
	F51B / 1313B	Three pieces of flesh vertically.
	F51C / 1313C	◝ (F51) reversed.
	F52 / 1313D	Excrement. Det. in ḥs "excrement."
	F53 / 1313E	Divine rod with ⬚ (F7).
	G1 / 1313F	Egyptian vulture. Phono. ꜣ. In ꜣ "vulture.'

	G2 13140	Two Egyptian vultures. Phono 33. In m33 “see.”
	G3 13141	Combination of  (G1) and  (U1). Phono. in m3. In sm3wy “renew.”
	G4 13142	Buzzard. Phono. tyw.
	G5 13143	Falcon. Ideo. ḥrw “Horus.”
	G6 13144	Combination of  (G5) and  (S45). De.t in bik “falcon.”
	G6A 13145	Falcon on  (V30).
	G7 13146	Falcon on  (R12). Det. imn “Amun,” nsw “king,” divine. 1st sing. pro. i, wi, with divine speaker.
	G7A 13147	Falcon in boat. Ideo. nmty “Nemty”
	G7B 13148	Falcon in boat. Use as G7a.
	G8 13149	Falcon on 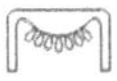 (S12). Ideo. Hr/bik nbw “Golden Horus/falcon.”

	G9 / 1314A	Falcon with ⊙ (N5) on head. Ideo. in rꜥ-ḥrw-3ḫty "Re-Horakhty."
	G10 / 1314B	Falcon in Sokar barque. Det. in skr "Sokar," ḥnw "Sokar bark."
	G11 / 1314C	Image of falcon. Det. in ꜥšm, ꜥḥm, ꜥḥm "divine image," šnbt "breast."
	G11A / 1314D	Image of falcon on ⎯ (R12).
	G12 / 1314E	Combination of (G11) and (S45). Use as G11.
	G13 / 1314F	Image of falcon with (S9). Ideo. ḥrw nḫny "Horus of Hierakonopolis." Det. in spdw "Sopdu."
	G14 / 13150	Vulture. Phono. mwt, mt. In mwt "mother."
	G15 / 13151	Combination of (G14) and (S45). Det. in mwt "Mut."
	G16 / 13152	Vulture and cobra each on ⌣ (V30). Ideo. in nbty "Two Ladies" (title of Pharaoh)
	G17 / 13153	Owl. Phono. m.

| | G18 | Two owls. |
| | 13154 | Phono. mm. |

| | G19 | Combination of (G17) and (D37). |
| | 13155 | Phono. mi, m. |

| | G20 | Combination of (G17) and (D36). |
| | 13156 | Use as G19. |

| | G20A | Combination of (G17) and (D21). |
| | 13157 | |

| | G21 | Guinea-fowl. |
| | 13158 | Phono. nḥ. In nḥḥ "eternity." |

| | G22 | Hoopoe. |
| | 13159 | Phono. ḏb/ḏbt. |

| | G23 | Lawping. |
| | 1315A | Det. and Ideo. in rḫyt "commoners." |

| | G24 | Lawping with twisted wings. |
| | 1315B | Use as G23. |

| | G25 | Northern bald ibis. |
| | 1315C | Phono. 3ḫ. In "spirit." |

| | G26 | Sacred ibis on (R12). |
| | 1315D | Det. in ḏḥwty "Thoth." |

	G26A / **1315E**	Sacred ibis. Use as G26.
	G27 / **1315F**	Flamingo. Phono. dšr. In dšr "red," "flamingo."
	G28 / **13160**	Glossy ibis. Phono. gm. In gmi "find."
	G29 / **13161**	Saddle-billed stork. Phono. b3. In "soul."
	G30 / **13162**	Three saddle-billed storks. Ideo. in b3w "spirits, strength."
	G31 / **13163**	Heron. Det. in šnty "heron."
	G32 / **13164**	Heron on perch. Det. or Ideo. in bʿḥi "inundated."
	G33 / **13165**	Cattle egret. Det. sd3 "tremble."
	G34 / **13166**	Ostrich. Det. in niw "ostrich."
	G35 / **13167**	Cormorant. Phono. ʿq. In ʿq "enter."

G36 13168	Swallow. Phono. wr. In wr "great."
G36A 13169	Swallow (low).
G37 1316A	Sparrow. Det. in nḏs "small," bin "bad."
G37A 1316B	Sparrow (low).
G38 1316C	White-fronted goose. Phono. gb. In gb "Geb." Det. in wf3 "talk," wsf "idle," ḥtm "perish."
G39 1316D	Pintail. Phono. s3. In s3 "son." Det. in si "duck."
G40 1316E	Pintail flying. Phono. p3. In p3 "the," "fly."
G41 1316F	Pintail alighting. Phono. ḫn. In ḫni "alight, halt," ḫn "speech," qm3 "throw," "create."
G42 13170	Widgeon. Det. and Ideo. in wš3 "fatten," ḏf3w "provisions."
G43 13171	Quail chick. Phono. w.

	G43A / 13172	Combination of (G43) and (X1).
	G44 / 13173	Two quail chicks. Phono. ww. In pḥww "end."
	G45 / 13174	Combination of (G43) and (D36). Phono wʿ. In wʿw "soldier."
	G45A / 13175	Combination of (G43) and (D37).
	G46 / 13176	Combination of (G43) and (U1). Phono. m3w.
	G47 / 13177	Duckling. Phono. t̠3. In t̠3y "male."
	G48 / 13178	Three ducklings in nest. Ideo. in sš "nest."
	G49 / 13179	Three ducklings in pool. Det. or Ideo. in sš "nest."
	G50 / 1317A	Two plovers. Ideo. for rḥty "washerman."
	G51 / 1317B	Bird pecking at fish. Det. in ḥ3m "catch fish."

	G52 / 1317C	Goose picking up grain. Det. in snm "feed."
	G53 / 1317D	Human-headed bird with ⚱ (R7). Ideo. in b3 "soul."
	G54 / 1317E	Plucked bird. Phono. snd̠. In snd̠ "fear."
	H1 / 1317F	Head of pintail. Ideo. in 3pd "bird." Det. in wšn "wring the neck of birds."
	H2 / 13180	Head of crested bird. Phono. m3ʿ, wšm, p3q. Det. in m3ʿ "temple of the head," "true."
	H3 / 13181	Head of spoonbill. Phono. p3q.
	H4 / 13182	Head of vulture. Phono. nr. Det. in nrt "vulture."
	H5 / 13183	Wing. Det. in d̠nḥ "wing."
	H6 / 13184	Feather. Phono. šw. Ideo. in šwt "feather." Det. and Ideo. in m3ʿt "truth."
	H6A / 13185	Hieratic feather.

| | H7 | Claw. |
| | 13186 | Phono. š3, š3t. In š3t "Shat" (location). |

| | H8 | Egg. |
| | 13187 | Ideo. in s3 "son." Det. sḥwt "egg." |

| | I1 | Gecko. |
| | 13188 | Phono. ʿš3. Det. for lizard. ex. ʿš3 "lizard" and ʿš3 "many, numerous." |

| | I2 | Turtle. |
| | 13189 | Det. or Ideo. for štyw "turtle." |

| | I3 | Crocodile. |
| | 1318A | Det. or Ideo. for crocodile. ex. msḥ "crocodile," 3d "agressive." Ideo. ity "sovereign," when reduplicated |

| | I4 | Crocodile on shrine. |
| | 1318B | Det. sbk "Sobek." |

| | I5 | Crocodile with curved tail. |
| | 1318C | Det. in s3q "collect, gather." |

| | I5A | Image of crocodile. |
| | 1318D | |

| | I6 | Crocodile scales. |
| | 1318E | Phono. km. In kmt "Egypt." |

| | I7 | Frog. |
| | 1318F | Det. in ḥqt "Heqet." Ideo. wḥm ʿnḫ "repeating life." |

| | I8 | Tadpole. |
| | 13190 | Det. ḥfnr "tadpole." Ideo. ḥfn "100,000." |

| | I9 | Horned viper. |
| | 13191 | Phono. f. Det. in it "father." |

| | I9A | Horned viper crawling out of enclosure. |
| | 13192 | |

| | I10 | Cobra. |
| | 13193 | Phono. ḏ. |

| | I10A | Cobra with feather. |
| | 13194 | |

| | I11 | Two cobras. |
| | 13195 | Phono ḏḏ. |

| | I11A | Combination of (I10), (X1) and (N18). |
| | 13196 | |

| | I12 | Erect cobra. |
| | 13197 | Det. in ꜥirt "uraeus." Det. of goddesses. |

| | I13 | Erect cobra on (V30). |
| | 13198 | Det. in w3ḏt "Wadjet." |

| | I14 | Snake. |
| | 13199 | Det. ḥf3w "snake, serpent." |

| | I15 | Snake. |
| | 1319A | Use as I14. |

| | K1 | Tilapia. |
| | 1319B | Phono. in. In int "bulti." |

| | K2 | Barbel. |
| | 1319C | Phono. bw. In bwt "abomination." |

| | K3 | Mullet. |
| | 1319D | Phono. ꜥd. In ꜥd-mr "district administrator." |

| | K4 | Elephant-snout fish. |
| | 1319E | Phono. ẖ3. In ẖ3t "oxyrhynchus." |

| | K5 | Petrocephalus bane. |
| | 1319F | Phono. bs. Det. in bsi "introduce." |

| | K6 | Fish scale. |
| | 131A0 | Det. and Ideo. in nšmt "fish scale." |

| | K7 | Puffer. |
| | 131A1 | Det. špt "discontented." |

| | K8 | Catfish. |
| | 131A2 | |

| | L1 | Dung beetle. |
| | 131A3 | Phono. ḫpr. In ḫpr "being, exist, become. |

	L2 131A4	Bee. Ideo. for bity "King of Lower Egypt."
	L2A 131A5	Combination of (M23), (L2) and two (X1).
	L3 131A6	Fly. Det. in ʿff "fly."
	L4 131A7	Locust. Det. in snḥm "locust."
	L5 131A8	Centipede. Det. sp3 "centipede."
	L6 131A9	Shell. Phono ḫ3. In ḫ3wt "offering table."
	L6A 131AA	(L6) reversed.
	L7 131AB	Scorpion. Det. and Ideo. in srqt "Selket."
	L8 131AC	Beetle.
	M1 131AD	Tree. Phono. im3. Det. nhwt, mnw "trees."

	M1A	Combination of (M1) and (M3).
	131AE	
	M1B	Combination of (M1) and (I9).
	131AF	
	M2	Plant.
	131B0	Phono. ḥn. In ḥni "rush," ḥnw "vessel." Det. in is "tomb."
	M3	Branch.
	131B1	Phono. ḫt. In ḫt "wood," ḫtyw "terrace," nḫt "strong."
	M3A	Combination of (G17) and (M3).
	131B2	
	M4	Palm branch.
	131B3	Ideo. in rnpt "year," ḥsbt "regnal year." Det. in tr "time."
	M5	Combination of (M4) and (X1).
	131B4	Det. or Ideo. in tr "time, season."
	M6	Combination of (M4) and (D21).
	131B5	Det. or Ideo. in tr "time, season."
	M7	Combination of (M4) and (Q3).
	131B6	Det. or Ideo. in rnpi "young."
	M8	Pool with lotus flowers.
	131B7	Phono š3. In š3 "marsh." Ideo. 3ḫt "Inundation" (season).

	M9 / **131B8**	Lotus flower. Det. or Ideo in sšn "lily."
	M10 / **131B9**	Lotus bud with straight stem. Det. in nḥbt "lily bud."
	M10A / **131BA**	Lotus bud with winding stem.
	M11 / **131BB**	Flower on long twisted stalk. Det. or Ideo. in wdn "offer."
	M12 / **131BC**	Lotus plant. Phono. ḫ3. In ḫ3w nw sšn "lily plants" ḫ3 "1,000," sḫ3 "remember."
	M12A / **131BD**	....
	M12B / **131BE**	....
	M12C / **131BF**	....
	M12D / **131C0**	....
	M12E / **131C1**	....

M12F	....	
131C2		
M12G	....	
131C3		
M12H	....	
131C4		
M13	Papyrus.	
131C5	Phono. w3ḏ, wḏ.	
M14	Combination of 𓇥 (M13) and 𓆓 (I10).	
131C6	Phono. w3ḏ. In w3ḏ wr "the sea."	
M15	Clump of papyrus with buds.	
131C7	Phono. 3ḫ. In 3ḫ-bit "Chemmis." Det. of Papyrus.	
M15A	Combination of 𓇭 (M15) and 𓊖 (O49).	
131C8		
M16	Clump of papyrus.	
131C9	Phono. ḥ3 . In ḥ3q "capture." Det. in "The Delta."	
M16A	Combination of 𓇯 (M16) and 𓊖 (O49).	
131CA		
M17	Reed.	
131CB	Phono. i. Phono. y, when doubled.	

	M17A	Two reeds.
	131CC	

	M18	Combination of 𓇋 (M17) and 𓂾 (D54).
	131CD	Phono i. In ii "come."

	M19	Heaped conical cakes between 𓇋 (M17) and 𓏏 (U36).
	131CE	Det. and Ideo. in ʿ3bt "offering."

	M20	Field of reeds.
	131CF	Det. sḫt "marshland," sm "occupation."

	M21	Reeds with root.
	131D0	Det. in sm "plant," "help."

	M22	Rush.
	131D1	Phono. nḫb . Phono. nn, when doubled. In nḫbt "germination," "Nehkbet."

	M22A	Two rushes.
	131D2	

	M23	Sedge.
	131D3	Phono. sw. Ideo. nswt "king."

	M24	Combination of 𓇓 (M23) and 𓂋 (D21).
	131D4	Ideo. rsw "south."

	M24A	Lily.
	131D5	

	M25 / 131D6	Combination of 🔣 (M26) and ⬭ (D21). Use as M24.
	M26 / 131D7	Flowering sedge. Phono. šmʿ. Ideo. šmʿw in "Upper Egypt."
	M27 / 131D8	Combination of 🔣 (M26) and ⬭ (D36). Phono. šmʿ.
	M28 / 131D9	Combination of 🔣 (M26) and ⬭ (V20). Ideo. in title wr mḏw šmʿw "Greatest of the tens of Upper Egypt."
	M28A / 131DA	Three lilies on ⊗ (O49).
	M29 / 131DB	Pod. Phono. nḏm. In nḏm "sweet.
	M30 / 131DC	Root. Det. or Ideo. bnr "sweet."
	M31 / 131DD	Rhizome. Det. in rd "grow."
	M31A / 131DE	⬭ (M1) in vase.
	M32 / 131DF	Rhizome. Use as M31

| | M33 | 3 grains horizontally. |
| | 131E0 | Ideo. in it "barley, corn." |

| | M33A | 3 grains vertically. |
| | 131E1 | |

| | M33B | 3 grains in triangular arrangement. |
| | 131E2 | |

| | M34 | Ear of emmer. |
| | 131E3 | Det. or Ideo. in bti "emmer." |

| | M35 | Heap of grain. |
| | 131E4 | Det. in ꜥḥꜥw "heaps." |

| | M36 | Bundle of flax showing bolls. |
| | 131E5 | Phono. ḏr. In ḏr "since," nḏri "hold fast." |

| | M37 | Bundle of flax. |
| | 131E6 | Phono. ḏr. |

| | M38 | Wide bundle of flax. |
| | 131E7 | Det. in mḥꜥ "flax," dm3 "bind together." |

| | M39 | Basket of fruit or grain. |
| | 131E8 | Det. in rnpt "vegetables." |

| | M40 | Bundle of reeds. |
| | 131E9 | Phono is. In is "tomb," iswt "crew." |

	M40A / 131EA	Bundle of reeds.
	M41 / 131EB	Piece of wood. Det. in ʿš "cedar."
	M42 / 131EC	Flower. Phono. wn. In wnm "eat," ḥwn "be young."
	M43 / 131ED	Vine on trellis. Det. or Ideo. in irp "wine."
	M44 / 131EE	Thorn. Det. spd "sharp."
	N1 / 131EF	Sky. Det. or Ideo. pt "sky," ḥrt "heaven," ḥry "above."
	N2 / 131F0	Sky with sceptre. Det. or Ideo. grḥ "night."
	N3 / 131F1	Sky with sceptre. Use as N2.
	N4 / 131F2	Sky with rain. Det. or Ideo. šnyt "rain," i3dt "dew."
	N5 / 131F3	Sun. Ideo. rʿ "sun, Re" hrw "day," sw "day."

| | N6 | Sun with uraeus. |
| | 131F4 | Det. or ideo in rꜥ "sun, Re." |

| | N7 | Combination of ⊙ (N5) and 🜂 (T28). |
| | 131F5 | Det. ẖrt-hrw "daytime." |

| | N8 | Sunshine. |
| | 131F6 | Phono. wbn. Det. or Ideo. ꜣḫw "sunshine," psḏ "shine," wbn "rise." |

| | N9 | Moon with lower half obscured. |
| | 131F7 | Phono. psḏ. In psḏt "Ennead." |

| | N10 | Moon with lower section obscured. |
| | 131F8 | Use as N9. |

| | N11 | Crescent moon. |
| | 131F9 | Ideo. ꜣbd "month." Det. iꜥḥ "moon." |

| | N12 | Crescent moon. |
| | 131FA | Det. iꜥḥ "moon." |

| | N13 | Combination of ⌒ (N11) and ✦ (N14). |
| | 131FB | Ideo. mḏdiwnt "half month festival." |

| | N14 | Star. |
| | 131FC | Phono. sbꜣ, dwꜣ. In sbꜣ "star," dwꜣ "morning." Ideo. wnwt "hour." |

| | N15 | Star in circle. |
| | 131FD | Ideo. in dwꜣt "netherworld." |

	N16 / 131FE	Land with grains. Phono. t3. In t3 "land, earth." Det. in ḏt "eternity."
	N17 / 131FF	Land. Use as N16.
	N18 / 13200	Sandy tract. Ideo. in iw "island."
	N18A / 13201	Combination of ____ (N18) and ____ (N35).
	N18B / 13202	Combination of ____ (X4B) and ____ (O34).
	N19 / 13203	Two sandy tracts. Ideo. in 3ḫt "horizon," ḥrw-3ḫty "Horakhty."
	N20 / 13204	Tongue of land. Phono. wḏb. In wḏb "shore." Det. in ḥ3b-sd "Sed Festival."
	N21 / 13205	Short tongue of land. Ideo. in idb "bank," idbwy "two banks."
	N22 / 13206	Broad tongue of land. Det. in ꜣḥt "field," sḫt "field."
	N23 / 13207	Irrigation canal. Det. in t3 "land," i3š "boundary."

| | N24 | Irrigation canal system. |
| | 13208 | Det. or Ideo. in sp3t "nome." |

| | N25 | Three hills. |
| | 13209 | Ideo. in ḫ3st "foreign land, hill country." |

| | N25A | Three hills (low). |
| | 1320A | |

| | N26 | Two hills. |
| | 1320B | Phono. ḏw "mountain." |

| | N27 | Sun over mountain. |
| | 1320C | Ideo. in 3ḫt "horizon." |

| | N28 | Rays of sun over hill. |
| | 1320D | Phono. ḫ'. In ḫ' "appear." |

| | N29 | Slope of hill. |
| | 1320E | Phono. q. |

| | N30 | Mound of earth. |
| | 1320F | Det. or Ideo. in i3t "mound." |

| | N31 | Road with shrubs. |
| | 13210 | Det. and Ideo. in w3t "road." |

| | N32 | Lump of clay. |
| | 13211 | Det. in sin "clay." |

○	**N33** 13212	Grain. Det. in nbw "gold."
○ ○ ○	**N33A** 13213	Three grains.
	N34 13214	Ingot of metal. Ideo. in bi3, ḥmt "copper."
	N34A 13215	Ingot of metal.
	N35 13216	Ripple of water. Phono. n.
	N35A 13217	Three ripples of water. Phono. mw. In mw "water."
	N36 13218	Canal. Phono. mr. In mr "canal."
	N37 13219	Pool. Phono. š. In š "pool."
	N37A 1321A	Pool.
	N38 1321B	Deep pool. Use as N37.

| | N39 | Pool with water. |
| | 1321C | Use as N37. |

| | N40 | Combination of ___ (N37) and ⋀ (D54). |
| | 1321D | Phono. šm. In šm "to go." |

| | N41 | Well with ripple of water. |
| | 1321E | Phono. ḥm. In ḥmt "wife." Det. in bi3 "copper." |

| | N42 | Well with line of water. |
| | 1321F | Use as N41. |

| | NL1 | Sign of first nome of Lower Egypt. |
| | 13220 | |

| | NL2 | Sign of second nome of Lower Egypt. |
| | 13221 | |

| | NL3 | Sign of third nome of Lower Egypt. |
| | 13222 | |

| | NL4 | Sign of fourth nome of Lower Egypt. |
| | 13223 | |

| | NL5 | Sign of fifth nome of Lower Egypt. |
| | 13224 | |

| | NL5A | Sign of fifth nome of Lower Egypt. |
| | 13225 | |

	NL6	Sign of sixth nome of Lower Egypt.
	13226	
	NL7	Sign of seventh nome of Lower Egypt.
	13227	
	NL8	Sign of eighth nome of Lower Egypt.
	13228	
	NL9	Sign of ninth nome of Lower Egypt.
	13229	
	NL10	Sign of tenth nome of Lower Egypt.
	1322A	
	NL11	Sign of eleventh nome of Lower Egypt.
	1322B	
	NL12	Sign of twelfth nome of Lower Egypt.
	1322C	
	NL13	Sign of thirteenth nome of Lower Egypt.
	1322D	
	NL14	Sign of fourteenth nome of Lower Egypt.
	1322E	
	NL15	Sign of fifteenth nome of Lower Egypt.
	1322F	

NL16	13230	Sign of sixteenth nome of Lower Egypt.
NL17	13231	Sign of seventeenth nome of Lower Egypt.
NL17A	13232	Sign of seventeenth nome of Lower Egypt.
NL18	13233	Sign of eighteenth nome of Lower Egypt.
NL19	13234	Sign of nineteenth nome of Lower Egypt.
NL20	13235	Sign of twentieth nome of Lower Egypt.
NU1	13236	Sign of first nome of Upper Egypt.
NU2	13237	Sign of second nome of Upper Egypt.
NU3	13238	Sign of third nome of Upper Egypt.
NU4	13239	Sign of fourth nome of Upper Egypt.

	NU5	1323A	Sign of fifth nome of Upper Egypt.
	NU6	1323B	Sign of sixth nome of Upper Egypt.
	NU7	1323C	Sign of seventh nome of Upper Egypt.
	NU8	1323D	Sign of eighth nome of Upper Egypt.
	NU9	1323E	Sign of ninth nome of Upper Egypt.
	NU10	1323F	Sign of tenth nome of Upper Egypt.
	NU10A	13240	Sign of tenth nome of Upper Egypt.
	NU11	13241	Sign of eleventh nome of Upper Egypt.
	NU11A	13242	Sign of eleventh nome of Upper Egypt.
	NU12	13243	Sign of twelfth nome of Upper Egypt.

	**NU13** / 13244	Sign of thirteenth nome of Upper Egypt.
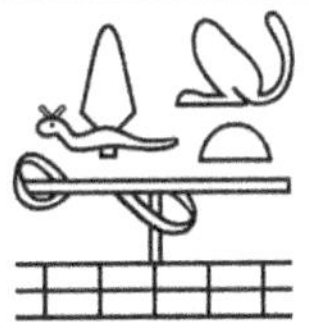	**NU14** / 13245	Sign of fourteenth nome of Upper Egypt.
	**NU15** / 13246	Sign of fifteenth nome of Upper Egypt.
	**NU16** / 13247	Sign of sixteenth nome of Upper Egypt.
	**NU17** / 13248	Sign of seventeenth nome of Upper Egypt.
	**NU18** / 13249	Sign of eighteenth nome of Upper Egypt.
	**NU18A** / 1324A	Sign of eighteenth nome of Upper Egypt.
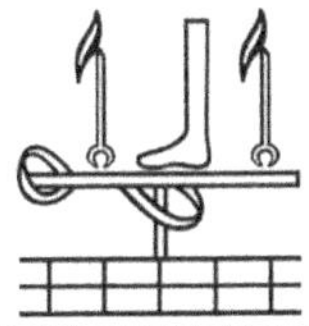	**NU19** / 1324B	Sign of nineteenth nome of Upper Egypt.
	**NU20** / 1324C	Sign of twentieth nome of Upper Egypt.
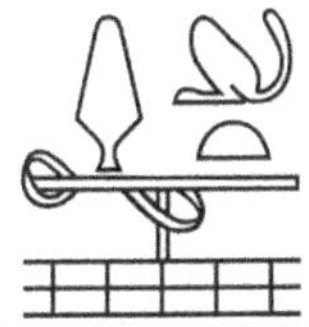	**NU21** / 1324D	Sign of twenty-first nome of Upper Egypt.

	NU22 / 1324E	Sign of twenty-second nome of Upper Egypt.
	NU22A / 1324F	Sign of second nome of Upper Egypt.
	O1 / 13250	House. Phono. pr. In pr "house," pri "go."
	O1A / 13251	Combination of ▭ (O1) and ☥ (S34).
	O2 / 13252	Combination of ▭ (O1) and ⸮ (T3). Ideo. in pr-ḥḏ "treasury."
	O3 / 13253	Combination of ▭ (O1), (P8), (X3), and (W22). Ideo. in prt-ḫrw "invocation offering."
	O4 / 13254	Shelter. Phono. h.
	O5 / 13255	Winding wall from upper-left corner. Phono. nm. In nmi "traverse."
	O5A / 13256	Winding wall from lower-left corner.
	O6 / 13257	Enclosure. Ideo. in ḥwt "temple, tomb, enclosure."

| | O6A | Opening of Hwt-enclosure. |
| | 13258 | |

| | O6B | Opening of Hwt-enclosure. |
| | 13259 | |

| | O6C | Opening of Hwt-enclosure. |
| | 1325A | |

| | O6D | Closing of Hwt-enclosure. |
| | 1325B | |

| | O6E | Closing of Hwt-enclosure. |
| | 1325C | |

| | O6F | Closing of Hwt-enclosure. |
| | 1325D | |

| | O7 | Combination of ▯ (O6) and ⌂ (X1). Use as O6. |
| | 1325E | |

| | O8 | Combination of ▯ (O7) and ⌐ (O29). Ideo. in ḥwt-ꜥ3 "Great temple, enclosure." |
| | 1325F | |

| | O9 | Combination of ▯ (O7) and ⌣ (V30). Ideo. in nbt-ḥyt "Nephthys." |
| | 13260 | |

| | O10 | Combination of ▯ (O6) and 𓅃 (G5). Ideo. in ḥwt-ḥrw "Hathor." |
| | 13261 | |

	O10A	Combination of ▯ (O6) and ♀ (S34).
	13262	
	O10B	Combination of ▯ (O6) and 🐝 (L2).
	13263	
	O10C	Combination of ▯ (O18) and 😐 (D2).
	13264	
	O11	Palace.
	13265	
	O12	Combination of ▯ (O11) and ╱ (D36).
	13266	Ideo. in ʿḥ "palace."
	O13	Battlemented enclosure.
	13267	Det. in sbḫ "enclose," sbḫt "gateway."
	O14	Part of battlemented enclosure.
	13268	Use as O13
	O15	Enclosure with ▽ (W10) and ◠ (X1).
	13269	Ideo. in wsḫt "hall."
	O16	Gateway with serpents.
	1326A	Det. or Ideo. in t3yt "curtain," t3yty "he of the curtain" (vizier title).
	O17	Open gateway with serpents.
	1326B	Use as O16

| | O18 | Shrine in profile. |
| | 1326C | Det. or Ideo. in k3r "shrine, chapel." |

| | O19 | Shrine with fence. |
| | 1326D | Det. in pr-wr "Great House." |

| | O19A | Shrine. |
| | 1326E | |

| | O20 | Shrine. |
| | 1326F | Det. in itrt "row of sanctuaries," ḫm "shrine." |

| | O20A | Shrine. |
| | 13270 | |

| | O21 | Façade of shrine. |
| | 13271 | Det. or Ideo. in sḥ-nṯr "divine shrine." |

| | O22 | Booth with pole. |
| | 13272 | Det. or Ideo. in sḥ "counsel," "booth." |

| | O23 | Double platform. |
| | 13273 | Ideo. in ḥ3b-sd "Sed Festival." |

| | O24 | Pyramid. |
| | 13274 | Det. in mr "pyramid." |

| | O24A | Pedestal of sun temple. |
| | 13275 | |

| | O25 | Obelisk. |
| | 13276 | Det. or Ideo. in t̠hn "obelisk." |

| | O25A | Obelisk and pedestal of sun temple. |
| | 13277 | |

| | O26 | Stela. |
| | 13278 | Det. or Ideo. in wd̠ "stela." |

| | O27 | Hall of columns. |
| | 13279 | Det. in h̠3 "office," h̠3wy "night." |

| | O28 | Column. |
| | 1327A | Phono iwn. In iwnw "Heliopolis," iwn "column." |

| | O29 | Horizontal wooden column. |
| | 1327B | Phono. ʿ3. In ʿ3 "great." |

| | O29A | Vertical wooden column. |
| | 1327C | Use as O29 |

| | O30 | Support. |
| | 1327D | Ideo. in sh̠nt "support." |

| | O30A | Four supports. |
| | 1327E | |

| | O31 | Door. |
| | 1327F | Det. in ʿ3 "door," sn, wn "open." |

	O32 13280	Gateway. Det. in sb3 "door," sbḫt "gateway."
	O33 13281	Façade of palace. Det. in srḫ "banner."
	O33A 13282	Closing of srx-enclosure.
	O34 13283	Bolt. Phono. s. In s "bolt."
	O35 13284	Combination of ⎯○⎯ (O34) and ⋀ (D54). Phono. s. In sbi "go," "perish," ms "bring."
	O36 13285	Wall. Ideo. in inb "wall."
	O36A 13286	Opening of oval fortified wall enclosure.
	O36B 13287	Closing of oval fortified wall enclosure.
	O36C 13288	Opening of square fortified wall enclosure.
	O36D 13289	Closure of square fortified wall enclosure.

	Sign	Unicode	Description
	O37	1328A	Falling wall. Det. in whn "overthrow," gs3 "tilt."
	O38	1328B	Corner of wall. Ideo. in qnbt "court, corner, magistrates."
	O39	1328C	Stone. Det. in inr "stone," dbni "deben (weight)," ḏbt "brick."
	O40	1328D	Stairway. Det. in rwd "stairwaway," ḫtyw "terrace."
	O41	1328E	Double stairway. Det. in q3y "high place," iʿr "ascend."
	O42	1328F	Fence. Phono. šsp. In šsp "receive."
	O43	13290	Low fence. Use as O42
	O44	13291	Emblem of Min. Ideo. in i3t "rank, office."
	O45	13292	Domed building. Det. or Ideo. in ipt "harim."
	O46	13293	Domed building. Use as O45.

| | O47 | Enclosed mound. |
| | 13294 | Ideo. in nḫn "Hierakonpolis." |

| | O48 | Enclosed mound. |
| | 13295 | Use as O47 |

| | O49 | Village. |
| | 13296 | Ideo. in niwt "town." |

| | O50 | Threshing floor. |
| | 13297 | Phono. sp. In sp "occasion, time, event," sp sn "two times." |

| | O50A | Hieratic threshing floor. |
| | 13298 | |

| | O50B | ☌ (O50A) reversed. |
| | 13299 | |

| | O51 | Pile of grain. |
| | 1329A | Det. or Ideo. in šnwt "granary." |

| | P1 | Boat. |
| | 1329B | Det. of boats. In dpt "ship," ḥ'w "ships," ḫdi "sail downstream." |

| | P1A | Boat upside down. |
| | 1329C | Det. in pnˁ "capsize." |

| | P2 | Ship under sail. |
| | 1329D | Det. in ḫnti "sail upstream." |

	P3 / 1329E	Sacred barque. Det. wi3 "sacred bark," ḏ3i "cross"
	P3A / 1329F	Sacred barque without steering oar.
	P4 / 132A0	Boat with net. Phono. wḥ'. In wḥ' "fisherman."
	P5 / 132A1	Sail. Det. or Ideo. in ṯ3w "wind, breath." Det. mḥyt "north wind."
	P6 / 132A2	Mast. Phono. 'ḥ'. In 'ḥ' "stand."
	P7 / 132A3	Combination of ☧ (P6) and ⌐ (D36). Use as P6.
	P8 / 132A4	Oar. Phono ḫrw. In m3' ḫrw "justified" ḫrw "voice," ḫrwy "enemy."
	P9 / 132A5	Combination of ⌇ (P8) and ⌐ (I9). Ideo for ḫr.fy "says, said."
	P10 / 132A6	Steering oar. Det. in ḥmw "steering oar," ḥmy "steerer"
	P11 / 132A7	Mooring post. Det. in mnit "mooring post."

| | Q1 | Seat. |
| | 132A8 | Phono. st, ws. In st "seat, place," wsir "Osiris," ḥtm "perish." |

| | Q2 | Portable seat. |
| | 132A9 | Phono. ws. In wsir "Osiris." |

| | Q3 | Stool. |
| | 132AA | Phono. p. |

| | Q4 | Head-rest. |
| | 132AB | Det. in wrs "headrest." |

| | Q5 | Chest. |
| | 132AC | Det. in hn "box," ꜥfdt "chest." |

| | Q6 | Coffin. |
| | 132AD | Det. or Ideo. in qrs "bury," qrsw "coffin." |

| | Q7 | Brazier. |
| | 132AE | Det. of fire. In ḫt "fire," sḏt "flame," srf "temperature." |

| | R1 | High table with offerings. |
| | 132AF | Det. or Ideo. in ḫ3t, ḫ3wt "offering table." |

| | R2 | Table with slices of bread. |
| | 132B0 | Use as R1. |

| | R2A | High table with offerings. |
| | 132B1 | |

	R3 / 132B2	Low table with offerings. Det. or Ideo. in wḏdw "offering table."
	R3A / 132B3	Low table.
	R3B / 132B4	Low table with offerings (simplified).
	R4 / 132B5	Loaf on mat. Phono. ḥtp. In ḥtp "altar, rest, be pleased."
	R5 / 132B6	Narrow censer. Det. or Ideo. in k3p "fumigate."
	R6 / 132B7	Broad censer. Use as R5
	R7 / 132B8	Bowl with smoke. Det. or Ideo. in sntr "incense."
	R8 / 132B9	Cloth on pole. Phono. nṯr. In nṯr "god."
	R9 / 132BA	Combination of (R8) and (V33). Det. or Ideo. in bd "incense."
	R10 / 132BB	Combination of (R8), (T28) and (N29). Ideo. in ḥrt-nṯr "necropolis."

| | R10A | Combination of ⌐ (R8) and ⌂ (T28). |
| 132BC | | |

| | R11 | Reed column. |
| 132BD | | Phono. ḏd. In ḏd "stable," ḏdw "Busiris." |

| | R12 | Standard. |
| 132BE | | Det. in i3t "standard." |

| | R13 | Falcon and feather on standard. |
| 132BF | | Ideo. in imnt "West," wnmi "right." |

| | R14 | Feather on standard. |
| 132C0 | | Ideo. in imnt "West," wnmi "right." |

| | R15 | Spear emblem. |
| 132C1 | | Ideo. in i3bt "East," i3by "left." |

| | R16 | Sceptre with feathers and string. |
| 132C2 | | Det. or Ideo in wḫ "Qus emblem." |

| | R16A | Sceptre with feathers. |
| 132C3 | | |

| | R17 | Wig on pole. |
| 132C4 | | Det. or Ideo. in t3-wr "This," "nome of Abydos." |

| | R18 | Combination of ⌐ (R17) and ▦ (N24). |
| 132C5 | | Use as R17 |

| | R19 | $\uparrow$ (S40) with feather. |
| | 132C6 | Det. in w3st "Thebes." |

| | R20 | Flower with horns. |
| | 132C7 | Ideo. in sšt "Seshat." |

| | R21 | Flower with horns. |
| | 132C8 | Use as R20. |

| | R22 | Two narrow belemnites. |
| | 132C9 | Phono. ḫm. In ḫm "shrine." With standard, Ideo. in mnw "Min." |

| | R23 | Two broad belemnites. |
| | 132CA | Use as R22 |

| | R24 | Two bows tied horizontally. |
| | 132CB | Det. in nit "Neith." |

| | R25 | Two bows tied vertically. |
| | 132CC | Use as R24. |

| | R26 | Combination of ▭ (N17), (F36), (M24A) and (M13). |
| | 132CD | |

| | R27 | Two arrows crossed over a shield. |
| | 132CE | |

| | R28 | Bat. |
| | 132CF | |

| | R29 | Niche with serpent. |
| | 132D0 | |

| | S1 | White crown.
Det. or Ideo. in ḥḏt "white crown." |
| | 132D1 | |

| | S2 | Combination of ⸮ (S1) and ⌣ (V30).
Det. or Ideo. in ḥḏt "white crown." |
| | 132D2 | |

| | S2A | Combination of ⸮ (S1) and ⊗ (O49). |
| | 132D3 | |

| | S3 | Red crown.
Phono. n. Det. or Ideo in dšrt "Red Crown." |
| | 132D4 | |

| | S4 | Combination of (S3) and ⌣ (V30).
Use as S3. |
| | 132D5 | |

| | S5 | Double crown.
Det. or Ideo. in sḫmty "double crown." |
| | 132D6 | |

| | S6 | Combination of (S5) and ⌣ (V30).
Use as S5. |
| | 132D7 | |

| | S6A | Combination of (S3) and ⊗ (O49). |
| | 132D8 | |

| | S7 | Blue crown.
Det. or Ideo. in ḫprš "blue crown." |
| | 132D9 | |

	S8 / 132DA	Atf-crown. Det. or Ideo. in 3tf "atef crown."
	S9 / 132DB	Two plumes. Det. or Ideo. in šwty "double plumes."
	S10 / 132DC	Headband. Phono mḏḥ. In mḏḥ "fillet."
	S11 / 132DD	Broad collar. Phono. wsḫ. In wsḫ "collar," swsḫ "widen."
	S12 / 132DE	Collar of beads. Det. or Ideo. in nbw "gold," ḥḏ "silver."
	S13 / 132DF	Combination of ▯ (S12) and ▯ (D58). Phono. nb.
	S14 / 132E0	Combination of ▯ (S12) and ▯ (T3). Ideo. in ḥḏ "silver."
	S14A / 132E1	Combination of ▯ (S12) and ▯ (S40). Ideo. in ḏʿm "electrum."
	S14B / 132E2	Combination of ▯ (S12) and ▯ (S40).
	S15 / 132E3	Pectoral. Det. or Ideo. in ṯhn "sparkle," ṯhnt "faience."

| | S16 | Pectoral. |
| | 132E4 | Use as S15. |

| | S17 | Pectoral. |
| | 132E5 | Use as S15 |

| | S17A | Girdle. |
| | 132E6 | |

| | S18 | Necklace with counterpoise. |
| | 132E7 | Det. or Ideo. in mnit "bead necklace." |

| | S19 | Necklace with seal from side. |
| | 132E8 | Ideo. in sd̲3wty "treasurer," sd̲3w "precious." Det. or Ideo. in ḫtm "seal." |

| | S20 | Necklace with seal from front. |
| | 132E9 | Ideo. in ḫtm "seal." |

| | S21 | Ring. |
| | 132EA | Det. in iwʿw, ʿʿw, sšw "ring." |

| | S22 | Shoulder-knot. |
| | 132EB | Phono. st̲. Det. or Ideo. in t3-wr "port." |

| | S23 | Knotted cloth. |
| | 132EC | Phono dmd̲. In dmd̲ "unite." |

| | S24 | Girdle knot. |
| | 132ED | Phono. t̲s. In t̲s "tie, bind." |

	S25	Garment with ties.
	132EE	Ideo. in iʿ3w "guide."
	S26	Apron.
	132EF	Det. or Ideo. in šndyt "apron."
	S26A	Apron.
	132F0	
	S26B	Apron.
	132F1	
	S27	Cloth with two strands.
	132F2	Det. or Ideo. in mnḫt "clothing."
	S28	Cloth with fringe on top and ∏ (S29).
	132F3	Det. in ḥbs "clothing," ḫ3p "conceal," kfi "uncover."
	S29	Folded cloth.
	132F4	Phono. s. In ʿnḫ.(w) (w)ḏ3 snb "may he live, be prosperous, be healthy." (L.P.H.)
	S30	Combination of ∏ (S29) and ⟋ (I9).
	132F5	Phono. sf. In sf "yesterday."
	S31	Combination of ∏ (S29) and ⟋ (U1).
	132F6	Phono. sm3. In sm3 "fighting bull."
	S32	Cloth with fringe on the side.
	132F7	Phono. si3. In si3t "fringed cloth."

| | S33 | Sandle. |
| | 132F8 | Ideo. in ṯbt "sandal," ṯbw "sandal maker." |

| | S34 | Sandle-strap. |
| | 132F9 | Phono. ʿnḫ. In ʿnḫ "live," ʿnḫ "sandal strap." |

| | S35 | Sunshade. |
| | 132FA | Ideo. in šwt "shadow, shade." |

| | S35A | Sunshade. |
| | 132FB | |

| | S36 | Sunshade. |
| | 132FC | Use as S35 |

| | S37 | Fan. |
| | 132FD | Det. or Ideo. in ḫw "fan." |

| | S38 | Crook. |
| | 132FE | Phono. ḥq3. In ḥq3 "rule," ḥq3t "scepter." |

| | S39 | Shepherd's crook. |
| | 132FF | Phono ʿwt. In ʿwt "flock." |

| | S40 | Sceptre. |
| | 13300 | Phono. w3s. In w3s "w3s-scepter." Ideo. in i3tt "milk, cream." |

| | S41 | Sceptre with spiral shaft. |
| | 13301 | Phono. ḏʿm. In ḏʿm "fine gold." |

| | S42 | Sceptre of authority. |
| | 13302 | Phono. sḫm. In sḫm "have power," sḫm "scepter." Det. or Ideo. in ḫrp "manage, at head." |

| | S43 | Walking stick. |
| | 13303 | Phono. md. In mdw "speak." |

| | S44 | Walking stick with /\ (S45). |
| | 13304 | Det. or Ideo. in 3ms "staff." |

| | S45 | Flagellum. |
| | 13305 | Det. or Ideo. in nḫ3ḫ3w "flail." |

| | S46 | Covering for head and neck. |
| | 13306 | |

| | T1 | Mace with flat head. |
| | 13307 | Phono. mn. In mnw "mace." |

| | T2 | Mace with round head diagonally. |
| | 13308 | Det. in sqr, sqri "smite." |

| | T3 | Mace with round head vertically. |
| | 13309 | Phono. ḥḏ. In ḥḏ "mace," ḥḏ "white, bright," ḥḏi "damage." |

| | T3A | Combination of ⌠ (T3) and ⌣ (N26). |
| | 1330A | |

| | T4 | Mace with strap. |
| | 1330B | Use as T3 |

T5 1330C	Combination of ⧖ (T3) and ⧖ (I10). Phono. ḥḏ.
T6 1330D	Combination of ⧖ (T3) and two ⧖ (I10). Phono. ḥḏḏ.
T7 1330E	Axe. Det. in mibt, minb "axe," mdḫ "hew."
T7A 1330F	Axe. Det. of 3qḥw "axe."
T8 13310	Dagger. Phono. tp. In tpy "first, chief, upon."
T8A 13311	Dagger. Det. in b3gsw "dagger."
T9 13312	Bow. Phono. pd/pḏ, in pd "stretch," pḏt "bow."
T9A 13313	Bow. Use as T9
T10 13314	Composite bow. Use as T9
T11 13315	Arrow. Phono. swn. In swn "perish," swnt "physician."

	T11A / **13316**	Two crossed arrows.
	T12 / **13317**	Bow-string. Phono. rwd/rwḏ. In rwd "hard, firm." Ideo. in ḏr "subdue."
	T13 / **13318**	Joined pieces of wood. Phono. rs. In rs "wakeful."
	T14 / **13319**	Throw stick vertically. Det. of "foreign." Ideo. in ʿ3m "Asiatics," ṯhnw "Libya." Det. in qm3 "create," qm3i "create."
	T15 / **1331A**	Throw stick slanted. Use as T14
	T16 / **1331B**	Scimitar. Det. in ḫpš "scimitar."
	T16A / **1331C**	Scimitar.
	T17 / **1331D**	Chariot. Det. or Ideo. in wrrt "chariot."
	T18 / **1331E**	Crook with package attached. Phono. šms. In šms "follow, accompany."
	T19 / **1331F**	Harpoon head. Phono. qs. In qs "annoy," qrs "bury." Det. in twr "pure."

| | T20 | Harpoon head. |
| | 13320 | Use as T19 |

| | T21 | Harpoon. |
| | 13321 | Phono. in wꜥ. In wꜥ "one." |

| | T22 | Arrowhead. |
| | 13322 | Phono. sn. In sn "brother," sn "smell." |

| | T23 | Arrowhead. |
| | 13323 | Use as T22 |

| | T24 | Fishing-net. |
| | 13324 | Phono. ꜥḥ/iḥ . In iḥ "net." |

| | T25 | Floats. |
| | 13325 | Phono. db3/ḏb3. In ḏb3 "adorn," db3 "replace." |

| | T26 | Bird-trap. |
| | 13326 | Det. or Ideo. in sḫt "trap, snare." |

| | T27 | Bird-trap. |
| | 13327 | Use as T26 |

| | T28 | Butcher's block. |
| | 13328 | Phono. ẖr. In ẖr "under," ẖrt "portion." |

| | T29 | Combination of ◝ (T30) and ⋀ (T28). |
| | 13329 | Ideo. in nmt "place of slaughter." |

| | T30 | Knife. |
| | 1332A | Ideo. for dmt "knife." Det. in dm "be sharp." |

| | T31 | Knife-sharpener. |
| | 1332B | Phono sšm. In sšm "guide, lead." |

| | T32 | Combination of (T31) and (D54). |
| | 1332C | Phono sšm. In sšm "guide, lead." |

| | T32A | Combination of (T31) and (S29). |
| | 1332D | |

| | T33 | Knife-sharpener of butcher. |
| | 1332E | Ideo. in sšm "butcher." |

| | T33A | Combination of (T33) and (S29). |
| | 1332F | |

| | T34 | Butcher's knife. |
| | 13330 | Phono. nm. In nm "knife," ẖnms "friend." |

| | T35 | Butcher's knife. |
| | 13331 | Use as T34 |

| | T36 | Shield. |
| | 13332 | |

| | U1 | Sickle. |
| | 13333 | Phono. m3. In m33 "see," 3sẖ "reap." |

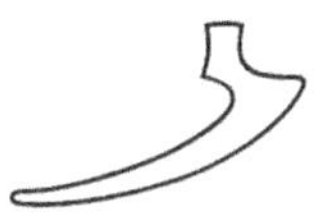	U2	13334	Sickle (low). Use as U1.
	U3	13335	Combination of 𓌳 (U1) and 𓁹 (D4). Phono. m3. In m33 “see.”
	U4	13336	Combination of 𓌳 (U1) and 𓐙 (AA11). Phono. m3ʿ. In m3ʿ “true.”
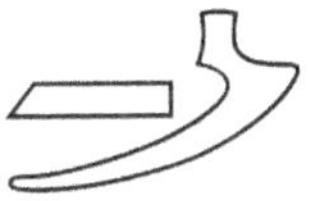	U5	13337	Combination of 𓌴 (U2) and 𓐙 (AA11). Use as U4.
	U6	13338	Diagonal hoe. Phono. mr. In mri “love.”
	U6A	13339	Vertical hoe.
	U6B	1333A	𓌹 (U6A) reversed.
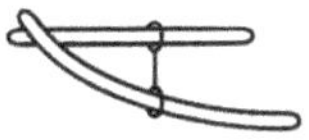	U7	1333B	Horizontal hoe. Use as U6.
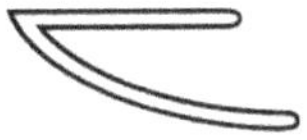	U8	1333C	Hoe without connecting rope. Phono. ḥn. In ḥn “hoe.”
	U9	1333D	Grain-measure with grain. Det. in bdt “emmer,” ẖ3i “measure,” ḥq3t “hekat measure.”

	U10 / **1333E**	▱ (U9) beneath ⸿ (M33). Ideo. in it "barley."
	U11 / **1333F**	Combination of ⸏ (S38) and ▱ (U9). Ideo. in ḥq3t "hekat measure."
	U12 / **13340**	Combination of ⸍ (D50) and ▱ (U9). Ideo. in ḥq3t "hekat measure."
	U13 / **13341**	Plough. Phono. šnʿ. In šnʿ "repel." Phono hb. In hb "plow."
	U14 / **13342**	Two joined branches. Phono. šnʿ. In šnʿ "repel."
	U15 / **13343**	Sledge. Phono. tm. In tm "be complete," ḥtm "perish."
	U16 / **13344**	Sledge with head of jackal. Det. in bi3 "wonder."
	U17 / **13345**	Pick in ground. Phono. grg. In grg "establish, snare," grg "falshood, lie."
	U18 / **13346**	Pick in basin. Use as U17.
	U19 / **13347**	Adze. Phono. nw. In nw "this."

	U20 13348	Adze. Use as U19
	U21 13349	Adze on wood. Phono. stp/sṯp. In stp "choose."
	U22 1334A	Chisel. Det. in mnḫ "efficient," mnḫ "carve."
	U23 1334B	Chisel. Phono. mr. In mr "ill," smr "friend." Phono. 3b. In 3bi "desire."
	U23A 1334C	Chisel.
	U24 1334D	Drill for stone. Ideo. in ḥmt "craft, art."
	U25 1334E	Drill for stone. Use as U24.
	U26 1334F	Drill for beads. Ideo. in wb3 "open."
	U27 13350	Drill for beads. Use as U26.
	U28 13351	Fire-drill. Phono. ḏ3. In ʿnḫ.(w) (w)ḏ3 snb "may he live, be prosperous, be healthy." (L.P.H.)

	U29 / 13352	Fire-drill. Use as U28.
	U29A / 13353	Fire-drill with string.
	U30 / 13354	Kiln. Phono. t3. In št3 "hot," t3 "mysterious.
	U31 / 13355	Baker's rake. Det. or Ideo. in rtḫty "baker," rtḫ "restrain."
	U32 / 13356	Pestle and mortar. Det. in smn "press down," smn "establish."
	U32A / 13357	Hieratic pestle and mortar.
	U33 / 13358	Pestle. Phono. ti.
	U34 / 13359	Spindle. Phono. ḫsf. In ḫsf "repel."
	U35 / 1335A	Combination of (U34) and (I9). Phono. ḫsf.
	U36 / 1335B	Club. Phono. ḥm. In ḥm "slave," ḥm "Majesty."

| | U37 | Razor. |
| | 1335C | Det. in ẖʿq "shave." |

| | U38 | Balance. |
| | 1335D | Det. or Ideo. in mḫ3t "scale." |

| | U39 | Post of balance. |
| | 1335E | Det. in wsṯt "post," wṯs, ṯsi "raise, lift." |

| | U40 | Hieratic post of balance. |
| | 1335F | Use as U39 |

| | U41 | Plummet. |
| | 13360 | Det. in tḫ "plumb bob." |

| | U42 | Pitchfork. |
| | 13361 | |

| | V1 | Coil of rope. |
| | 13362 | Phono. šn. In šnt "dispute," šni "litigate," št "hundred." |

| | V1A | .... |
| | 13363 | |

| | V1B | .... |
| | 13364 | |

| | V1C | .... |
| | 13365 | |

| | V1D | .... |
| 13366 | |

| | V1E | .... |
| 13367 | |

| | V1F | .... |
| 13368 | |

| | V1G | .... |
| 13369 | |

| | V1H | .... |
| 1336A | |

| | V1I | .... |
| 1336B | |

| | V2 | Combination of ___ (O34) and ⟑ (V1). Det. in st3 "drag." Ideo. in st̲3t "aurora." |
| 1336C | |

| | V2A | Hieratic form of ⟑ (V2). |
| 1336D | |

| | V3 | Combination of ___ (O34) and three ⟑ (V1). Ideo. in r-st̲3w "necropolis." |
| 1336E | |

| | V4 | Lasso. Phono. w3. In w3ḥ "endure." |
| 1336F | |

| | V5 | Looped rope. |
| | 13370 | Det. or Ideo. in snṯ "plot." |

| | V6 | Cord with ends upward. |
| | 13371 | Phono. šs, šsr. |

| | V7 | Cord with ends downward. |
| | 13372 | Phono. šn. |

| | V7A | Cord with ends downward. |
| | 13373 | |

| | V7B | Hieratic cord with ends downward. |
| | 13374 | |

| | V8 | Cord downward. |
| | 13375 | Use as V7 |

| | V9 | Round cartouche. |
| | 13376 | Det. in šnw "cartouche." |

| | V10 | Oval cartouche. |
| | 13377 | Det. in šnw "cartouche," rn "name. |

| | V11 | End of cartouche. |
| | 13378 | Det. in dni "restrain, dam," pḫ3 "split. |

| | V11A | Opening of cartouche. |
| | 13379 | |

	V11B	Closing of cartouche.
	1337A	
	V11C	Closing of knotless cartouche.
	1337B	
	V12	String.
	1337C	Det. in sšd "headband," fḫ "loosen," fḫnw "Phoenicians."
	V12A	String.
	1337D	
	V12B	String.
	1337E	
	V13	Rope.
	1337F	Phono. ṯ.
	V14	Rope with tick.
	13380	Use as last.
	V15	Combination of ⚊ (V13) and ⋀ (D54).
	13381	Phono. iṯ. In iṯi "seize."
	V16	Looped cord.
	13382	Phono. s3. In s3 "protection."
	V17	Shelter of papyrus.
	13383	Ideo. in s3 "protection."

	V18	Shelter of papyrus.
	13384	Use as V17
	V19	Hobble with cross-bar.
	13385	Det. in mdt "stable," k3r "shrine," tm3 "mat."
	V20	Hobble.
	13386	Phono. md. In mdwt "stables," md "10."
	V20A	....
	13387	
	V20B	....
	13388	
	V20C	....
	13389	
	V20D	....
	1338A	
	V20E	....
	1338B	
	V20F	....
	1338C	
	V20G	....
	1338D	

	V20H	....
	1338E	
	V20I	....
	1338F	
	V20J	....
	13390	
	V20K	....
	13391	
	V20L	....
	13392	
	V21	Combination of ⌒ (V20) and ⌐ (I10). Phono. mḏ.
	13393	
	V22	Whip. Phono. mḥ. In mḥ "fill."
	13394	
	V23	Whip. Use as V22.
	13395	
	V23A	Whip.
	13396	
	V24	Cord on stick. Phono. wḏ. In wḏ "command, decree."
	13397	

| | V25 | Cord on stick with tick. |
| | 13398 | Use as V24 |

| | V26 | Netting needle. |
| | 13399 | Phono. ꜥd/ꜥḏ. In ꜥd "good condition." |

| | V27 | Netting needle. |
| | 1339A | Use as V26. |

| | V28 | Wick. |
| | 1339B | Phono. ḥ. |

| | V28A | Combination of ⸢V28⸣ (V28) and ⸢D36⸣ (D36). |
| | 1339C | |

| | V29 | Swab. |
| | 1339D | Phono. w3ḥ, sk. |

| | V29A | Combination of ⸢V29⸣ (V29) and ⸢V31⸣ (V31). |
| | 1339E | |

| | V30 | Basket. |
| | 1339F | Phono. nb. In nb "lord," nb "every, all." |

| | V30A | Basket (low). |
| | 133A0 | |

| | V31 | Basket with right handle. |
| | 133A1 | Phono k. |

	V31A	133A2	Basket with left handle. Use as V31.
	V32	133A3	Frail. Phono. msn. In msn "Mesen." Det. in g3wt "bundles," g3w "absence, lack."
	V33	133A4	Bag. Det. in šsr "linen."
	V33A	133A5	Bundle.
	V34	133A6	Bag. Use as V33.
	V35	133A7	Bag. Use as V33.
	V36	133A8	Receptacle. Phono. ḥn. In ḥnt "occupation."
	V37	133A9	Bandage. Det. or Ideo. in idr "bandage, bind," idr "herd."
	V37A	133AA	Bandage.
	V38	133AB	Bandage. Det. in wt "bandage."

| | V39 | Knot-amulet. |
| | 133AC | Ideo. in tit "Isis knot." |

| | V40 | Hobble on its side. |
| | 133AD | |

| | V40A | Two hobbles on their side. |
| | 133AE | |

| | W1 | Oil jar with ties. |
| | 133AF | Det. in mḏt "ointment," mrḥt "oil." |

| | W2 | Oil jar. |
| | 133B0 | Phono. b3s. In b3stt "Bastet," b3s "oil jar." |

| | W3 | Alabaster basin. |
| | 133B1 | Det. or Ideo. in ḥb "feast," ḥb "mourn." |

| | W3A | Alabaster basin (low). |
| | 133B2 | |

| | W4 | Combination of (O22) and (W3). |
| | 133B3 | Det. or Ideo. in ḥb "feast," tp-rnpt "feat of the first of the year." |

| | W5 | Combination of (T28) and (W3). |
| | 133B4 | Ideo in ẖry-ḥbt "lector priest." |

| | W6 | Metal vessel. |
| | 133B5 | Det. in wḥt "cauldron." |

W7 / 133B6	Granite bowl.	Det. in 3bt "family," m3t "proclaim."
W8 / 133B7	Deformed granite bowl.	Use as W7.
W9 / 133B8	Jug with left handle.	Phono. ḫnm.
W9A / 133B9	Jug with right handle.	
W10 / 133BA	Cup.	Phono. ḥnw. In ḥnwt "mistress." Det. or Ideo. in wsḫ "wide."
W10A / 133BB	Pot with tick.	Phono. b3.
W11 / 133BC	Round ring stand.	Phono. g. Det. or Ideo. in nst "throne."
W12 / 133BD	Square ring stand.	Use as W11.
W13 / 133BE	Earthenware pot.	Det. or Ideo. in dšrt "red pot."
W14 / 133BF	Water jar.	Phono. ḥs. In ḥst "water jar."

	W14A	Combination of 𓐍 (V28), 𓏌 (W14) and 〰 (O34).
	133C0	
	W15	Water jar with water.
	133C1	Det. or Ideo. in qbb, qbḥ "cool, water."
	W16	Water jar with water in ring stand.
	133C2	Use as W15.
	W17	Three water jars in rack.
	133C3	Phono. ḫnt. In ḫntw "jar rack."
	W17A	Three water jars in rack (simplified).
	133C4	
	W18	Four water jars in rack.
	133C5	Use as W17
	W18A	Four water jars in rack (simplified).
	133C6	
	W19	Milk jug in net.
	133C7	Phono. mi. In mi "likeness."
	W20	Milk jug with leaf.
	133C8	Det. in irtt "milk."
	W21	Twin wine jars.
	133C9	Det. in irp "wine."

	W22 / 133CA	Beer jug. Ideo. in ḥnqt "beer." Det. in qrḥt "vessel."
	W23 / 133CB	Jar with handles. Use as W22.
	W24 / 133CC	Bowl. Phono. nw, in, ink.
	W24A / 133CD	Three bowls.
	W25 / 133CE	Combination of ○ (W24) and ⋀ (D54). Phono. in. In ini "fetch, bring."
	X1 / 133CF	Flat loaf. Phono. t. Ideo. in t "bread."
	X2 / 133D0	Tall loaf. Det. of bread. In t "bread." Ideo. in dḥwty "Thoth."
	X3 / 133D1	Tall loaf. Use as X2
	X4 / 133D2	Roll of bread. Det. in sni "pass by," fq3 "cake."
	X4A / 133D3	Roll of bread.

	X4B / 133D4	Roll of bread.
	X5 / 133D5	Hieratic roll of bread. Det. in ʿqw "provisions."
	X6 / 133D6	Round loaf. Det. in p3t "loaf."
	X6A / 133D7	Round loaf.
	X7 / 133D8	Half-loaf. Det. in snw "offerings." When doubled, wnm "eat."
	X8 / 133D9	Conical loaf. Phono. di. In rdi "give."
	X8A / 133DA	Hieratic conical loaf.
	Y1 / 133DB	Scroll with ties. Phono. mḏ3t. Ideo. in mḏ3t "paypyrus roll, book." Det. in rḫ "know."
	Y1A / 133DC	Vertical scroll with ties. Use as Y1
	Y2 / 133DD	Scroll. Use as Y1

| | Y3 | Scribe's outfit with palette on left. |
| | 133DE | Det. or Ideo. in sš "write," nˁˁ "smooth." |

| | Y4 | Scribe's outfit with palette on right. |
| | 133DF | Use as Y3 |

| | Y5 | Game board. |
| | 133E0 | Phono. mn. In imn "Amun" mn "remain." |

| | Y6 | Game piece. |
| | 133E1 | Det. or Ideo. in ib3 "game piece," "dance." |

| | Y7 | Harp. |
| | 133E2 | Det. in bnt "harp." |

| | Y8 | Sistrum. |
| | 133E3 | Det. in sššt "sistrum." |

| | Z1 | Stroke. |
| | 133E4 | Follows Ideograms. Det. wˁ "one." Ideo. numerals 1-9. |

| | Z2 | Three 〡 (Z1) horizontally. |
| | 133E5 | Det. of plurality. |

| | Z2A | Three 〡 (Z1) horizontally. |
| | 133E6 | |

| | Z2B | Three ○ (D67) horizontally. |
| | 133E7 | |

	Z2C	Three 〡 (Z1) in triangular arrangement.
	133E8	
	Z2D	Three 〡 (Z1) in triangular arrangement.
	133E9	
	Z3	Three 〡 (Z1) vertically.
	133EA	Same as Z2.
	Z3A	Three lying 〡 (Z1) vertically.
	133EB	Same as Z2.
	Z3B	Three ο (D67) vertically.
	133EC	
	Z4	Two diagonal strokes.
	133ED	Det. Duality
	Z4A	Two 〡 (Z1) horizontally.
	133EE	Det. Duality.
	Z5	Curved diagonal stroke.
	133EF	Replacement for complex or dangerous signs, human figures.
	Z5A	Diagonal stroke.
	133F0	
	Z6	Hieratic substitute for (A13) or (A14).
	133F1	Det. in m(w)t "die"

	Z7 / 133F2	Hieratic quail chick. Phono. w.
	Z8 / 133F3	Oval. Det. of round.
	Z9 / 133F4	Diagonal cross. Phono. sw3. In sw3 "pass."
	Z10 / 133F5	Wide diagonal cross. Use as Z9.
	Z11 / 133F6	Cross. Phono. im. In imy "who is in."
	Z12 / 133F7	Hieratic striking man.
	Z13 / 133F8	Circle.
	Z14 / 133F9	Indeterminable hieratic tick.
	Z15 / 133FA	Long vertical stroke.
	Z15A / 133FB	....

	Z15B	.....
	133FC	
	Z15C	.....
	133FD	
	Z15D	.....
	133FE	
	Z15E	.....
	133FF	
	Z15F	.....
	13400	
	Z15G	.....
	13401	
	Z15H	.....
	13402	
	Z15I	.....
	13403	
	Z16	Long horizontal stroke.
	13404	
	Z16A	.....
	13405	

	Z16B	....
	13406	
	Z16C	....
	13407	
	Z16D	....
	13408	
	Z16E	....
	13409	
	Z16F	....
	1340A	
	Z16G	....
	1340B	
	Z16H	....
	1340C	
	AA1	Basket from above.
	1340D	Phono. ḫ.
	AA2	Pustule.
	1340E	Det. in bodily growths or conditions.
	AA3	Pustule with liquid.
	1340F	Use as Aa2.

| | AA4 | Pot with two ticks. |
| | 13410 | Var. of W10a. |

| | AA5 | Navigation instrument. |
| | 13411 | Phono. ḥp. |

| | AA6 | Instrument. |
| | 13412 | Det. in tm3 "mat." |

| | AA7 | Instrument. |
| | 13413 | Det. in sqr "smite." |

| | AA7A | (AA7) reversed. |
| | 13414 | |

| | AA7B | Later equivalent of (AA7). |
| | 13415 | |

| | AA8 | Irrigation canal. |
| | 13416 | Phono. qn. In qn "complete." |

| | AA9 | Instrument. |
| | 13417 | Det. in ḫwd "rich." |

| | AA10 | Unknown. |
| | 13418 | Det. in drf "writing." |

| | AA11 | Platform. |
| | 13419 | Phono. m3ꜥ. |

	AA12 / **1341A**	Platform. Use as Aa11.
	AA13 / **1341B**	Sharp half. Phono. im, m.
	AA14 / **1341C**	Bent half. Phono. im, m.
	AA15 / **1341D**	Blunt half. Phono. im, m.
	AA16 / **1341E**	Short half. Phono. gs. In gs "side, half."
	AA17 / **1341F**	Lid. Phono. s3. In s3 "back."
	AA18 / **13420**	Square lid. Use as Aa17
	AA19 / **13421**	Instrument. Det. in ḥr "prepare," ḥryt "dread."
	AA20 / **13422**	Bag. Phono. ʿpr. In ʿpr "equip."
	AA21 / **13423**	Instrument. Phono. wḏʿ. In wḏʿ "judge."

AA22	13424	Combination of ⌗ (AA21) and ⌐ (D36). Use as Aa21.
AA23	13425	High warp between stakes. Det. in mḏd "puncture, press, adhere."
AA24	13426	Low warp between stakes. Use as Aa23.
AA25	13427	Unknown. Ideo. in sm3 "stolist" (priestly title).
AA26	13428	Unknown. Det. in sbi "rebel."
AA27	13429	Spindle. Phono. nḏ. In nḏ "ask, inquire."
AA28	1342A	Level. Phono. qd. In qd "build."
AA29	1342B	Instrument. Use as Aa28.
AA30	1342C	Frieze. Det. in ḫqr "adorn."
AA31	1342D	Frieze. Use as Aa30.

	AA32	Archaic bow.
	1342E